For anyone who needs to be heard — I hear you.

Warning: Some of the content in this book can get graphic. Take care of yourself. This book is put together in its most raw form for the sole purpose of showing people they are not alone and things DO get better. Together, we can get through this crazy thing they call life. You are not alone.

This is a compilation of thoughts starting from the beginning of the madness through recovery. Writing out what I was feeling helped me get it off my chest little by little. Only a couple friends knew I was going through something, but nobody understood what it was, including me. These pages contain raw, unedited thoughts that help to tell my story.

My mental health journey began in 2010. From the outside, I was living a picture perfect life. However, that was not how I felt. I was always tired, angry, sad, and overall just very dazed. I didn't know what it was or why I was feeling this way. All I knew was that I was no longer just like my friends — And not in a good way.

In 2010, I was a freshman in high school. I was working towards earning my First Degree Black Belt, which I then received in August of 2011. I was in the best shape of my life. I earned a varsity letter for the school's soccer team in just my first year. Freshman year was turning out to be the best and worst year of my life. I did well in school and was involved in many different clubs. I had great friends and teammates.

My parents were married and healthy. My grandparents were my best friends and I loved to visit their house, which we did often. Most of my family was local and very involved in my life. There was no reason to feel anything but proud, happy, and grateful for my life. However, that's when my story began.

Table of Contents

Love Anything, Because You Can't Love Yourself

Happiness never felt easy until I met you.

Love Anything, Because You Can't Love Yourself

I'm not sure if I even know what love is yet,
but the feeling he gives me is a little something like sunshine.

My heart is happiest when it's next to yours.

Your love is like morphine to my soul.
You take all the pain away.

Beautifully.

With you and me, there's no need for fancies.

Who wants to be dreaming when we can make it a reality?

You're my own personal getaway.

Love Anything, Because You Can't Love Yourself

Those summer nights are what I'm going to miss. Laying under the stars. 70 degrees with a light summer breeze. The moonlight shining where we lay side by side.

The way you look into my eyes gives me chills. Almost as if I can feel us connecting in a way that is too hard to explain.

I lay awake thinking about you and our future together. I'd write a song about my love for you, but it doesn't even fit into words.

I think I'm falling for him.
Ever since the moment I laid eyes on him I knew he was a little something special.

I lay under the stars and sing songs that remind me of us.
His eyes make me melt, that sweet shade of blue. Oh it gets me, crazy.

Thoughts of you can't escape my head.
When I'm sleeping, my dreams are of you
and that gets me through the hard times.

When I look into his eyes, I see a happy world filled with happy things and for a second I actually feel happy. I think.

He holds my resiliency in the palm of his hand

...and that's not something I'm proud of.

I knew our love was wrong from the start, but I couldn't help listening to my heart.
You're like gravity and I can't fight the feeling I get when I'm with you.

You're comfy, but I don't love you with fire in my eyes
and passion in my chest.
I love you like cold pizza on a Saturday morning.
I love you like big sweaters in the dead of winter.
My love for you is only comfy.

Loving Things Was Not That Easy Anymore

Here we go again.

Another night with tear filled eyes.

Voices echo down the halls.

I know I've said it before, but I think I'm breaking down.

With every day that I grow, I feel as if every drop of happiness I hold is slowly dripping away.

You don't act like you want me here,
but it's just hard to say these things out loud.

And it was that day in the classroom, when the tears I used to hold back fell from my eyes. With a crack in my voice, I still managed to say

—I'm fine.

I think I let him hurt me because when he did,
I didn't have to call it self harm.
And if I self harm, that means I have depression.
So I don't have depression, right?

Wrong.

One day I ask you,

"Do you love me?"

And honestly I'm not sure if I want the real answer.

I need to stop this sick obsession.

It puts me through depression and I can't take the feeling I get when I see you with her.

Back when I thought that was what "caused" my depression...

Loving Things Was Not That Easy Anymore

I used to love those eyes of yours.
Dreams of you danced in my head.

Now when you look at me it feels as if we never touched,
never cared, and never laughed.
I'd like to say I have never felt anything for you,
but that's not true.

I want to end this.
I want to end us.
I don't want to think of the times we had, because it tears me
apart.

I don't know why I waste so much time clinging to the thought of you ever caring about me the way I do for you.

You killed what was left of the good in me.

All I do is sit here and hope that one day you'll see my worth and want to treat me better.

Loving Things Was Not That Easy Anymore

Sometimes you got me on cloud nine, but then we're back where
we began. I feel like I'm your moon, brightening up your night as
you orbit on your own.

Sometimes I want to lay my head, shut my eyes and try not to
think about you, but that only makes it worse. All I want to do is
make you happy, yet I'm dying inside.

In the end, if it came down to my last breath, I'd use it to say
I love you.

Back when I thought I knew what love was.

Nobody has ever been afraid of losing me, including myself.

Dating you taught me
that my body does not, in fact,
belong to the soul that lives within.

My body belongs to you.
Ever since "no" became too scary to say
and "yes" made my life a lot less complicated.
"Yes" stopped many late night fights and
prevented many (many) holes in those dorm room walls.
It became easier to rid myself of the
freedom to choose than to
simply say "no."

The scars are a reminder of what I've been through.

A finder of my strength to keep on going.

They keep me from breaking down.

I'm never going to be someone people always want to be around. Nobody sees sunshine in the eyes of the depressed girl.

They say love is patient. Love is kind.

But what about the love that breaks you
and leaves you stranded.

What about the love that leaves you gasping for air
or the love that makes you feel like you're dying.

Or the love that one day feels like summer
and the next is like a crashing tidal wave.

What about the love that leaves you wondering
late at night until the birds start chirping
and you pass out from pure exhaustion.

What about that love?

Loving Things Was Not That Easy Anymore

You hear the sadness in my voice before you can see it in my eyes.

For the past 8 hours I've been trying to decide which option will
end it the least amount of pain:
1.) Not speaking to you
2.) Speaking to you and being disappointed

I don't trust you.

Plain and simple.

It isn't because of anything you did.

When the beer touches your lips, I feel the ache of emptiness

as if you physically carved out my insides like a jack- o- lantern.

It feels like my insides have been ripped apart like the biggest

package on Christmas morning.

Again, not because of you.

I've been taught that an intoxicated man has no rules

and I have no meaning.

It's almost as if alcohol is a ticket to forgetting what you already

have at home.

Unfortunately, when you get me, you get all the damage other men

left behind.

Maybe I don't trust you because I know you deserve better.

You don't deserve to have to deal with the broken girl.

I don't deserve you.

Maybe it's because I know the girls you are talking to are better.

Happy.

I mean, their mental health allows them to have fun.

Must be nice.

Love would be so much easier if I was worthy of being someone's priority.

The beginning is always full of fun, love, and happiness. There is some of that in the middle too, but eventually he won't love you for you anymore. He will only love you for the security, the sense of being wanted, the parties, or the sex. He won't love you on the lazy Sunday mornings before you have brushed your teeth or the late nights after hard days at work. He won't love you for what is real. They never do.

One day I'll learn to love things the way I love the feeling of
warmth draining from my cuts.
One day I'll be able to tell you why some days I just can't answer
your calls.
One day I'll find someone who loves me the way I wish you would.
One day I'll have the confidence they talk about in songs.
One day I'll be happy with my life, with myself.
One day I'll be able to look up at the stars and not pray to join
them.
One day I'll look back and be able to say "look how far I've come."
But... just not today.

I miss the me I used to be.
I miss the life that life scared out of me.

I miss the me that wasn't afraid to be me.
I miss the me who wasn't afraid. *Period.*
The me who was who she was because
she didn't know to act any different.

Because why should she.

And The Days Just Keep Getting Worse

How can so much sadness fit into someone so "young and successful."

I used to think people who self-harmed were out of their mind.

That was back when life wasn't more painful than slicing thin

lines into my skin while sitting on the bathroom floor.

The second the cold blade touches my warm skin the pain melts

away.

Weird, right?

I know that isn't how I am supposed to feel,

but I do.

It's just that for those few seconds,

the only pain I feel is physical.

It's much better than the pain that lives inside my head

...or no feeling at all.

As memories fade, feelings change.
Without you, nothing is the same.

Don't let me believe this will only be a pointless memory.

Q: Is it even possible to be overwhelmed by a lack of feeling?

A: Yes, darling. That is a decadent mixture of what's called both depression and anxiety.

I've realized happy girls shine brighter
and I'll never shine like her.

For me, wanting to cut is just another part of most days.

Usually, I can ignore it and get through the day.

It's kinda like the feeling of being tired.

You can usually either ignore it or give in.

Only instead of getting a coffee or taking a nap to cope with the emptiness, it's putting a blade to my skin that just healed from the last time I was "tired."

Then there are those days the withdrawal body aches force my mind to crave it like any other person would crave chocolate cake straight from the oven, but that's what's normal for me.

Bleed your heart out on paper.
The deeper the cut the more you feel.
There isn't much left in me, but
I'd go empty for you.
I want to feel you until I can't anymore.

The feeling you gave me was hot,

and not in a good way.

Hot like the longest summer day with no water in sight.

Hot like fire consuming all the happy moments I thought we had.

Hot like a fever I tried desperately to sweat out.

I just remember the feeling of being horribly homesick.
Homesick for a place I haven't found to exist.

My mouth waters to the thought
of putting a blade to my skin.

Why is it that you can be having the time of your life
and all of a sudden
you want to die?

Nothing went wrong.
Everything is just perfect,
but you still want to die.

Why is that feeling like your ex you keep trying to forget?
I thought I broke up with that feeling.
I am better without you.

It is too much to ask for someone to love me for me?

I often wish I was someone else,

but I'm starting to realize how much that keeps

me from being me.

I haven't been myself for a few years now.

Maybe I'd like myself more if I started acting like me

and stopped comparing myself to others.

I'm sick of apologizing for being me.

When will I realize I don't have to try to be

anyone but myself?

The only problem is,

I'm not sure if I know who the real me is anymore.

Sometimes the only thing keeping me alive is the inability to get out of bed. At least in bed I'm alive and there is not much I can do to change that unless I get out of bed.

I think depression has made it hard for me to learn what love is.

What I Thought Was Recovery

Yes I began to laugh.

Yes I cracked a smile,

but the memories will be here awhile.

What I Thought Was Recovery

I wipe my tears as you walk by.

You have no idea what you do to me.

I will never forget that time.

That time when I couldn't hold it in anymore.

You looked into my eyes.

I couldn't help but let a tear slip by as you said, "what's wrong?"

I don't really know.

When I walk away I don't look back.

It feels like a heart attack, but I wouldn't let you see me like this.

What I Thought Was Recovery

I hate that your scent still lingers on my sheets.
It makes thoughts of you flood my mind and I feel like I'm
drowning.

You were what I thought my heart needed.
What I thought my heart "deserved."

In the end, you were the last thing anyone's heart deserves.
In the end, I was happier without you.

Those little white lines on your skin each have their own story.
A reason for living there upon your wrist.
It's not always easy.

They explain the actions that don't always make sense,
but there is nothing you can do to change the past.

What I Thought Was Recovery

Call me foolish.
Call me crazy,
but for some reason
I thought you were different.

I started to think the nicotine would create a better me, but
now you're all I can think about.

You'd never know though.
Only if you'd catch the liquor in my veins or if the words would
escape from my lips.
I don't want you to see what you did to me.

I'm excited for a life without you.

What I Thought Was Recovery

You're my guiding light
leading me where I'm supposed to be.
Right next to you.
With you next to me.

Whenever I'm lost and don't know what to do.
It's you who guides me through.

You saved me.

As you felt me losing my grip, you grabbed me by the torn up wrist and saved me.

People think I'm crazy, but they don't understand.

The way I see it, things are much too hard for you to comprehend, but that didn't matter.

He made me feel the safest when I was with him.

Yet, it was always his hands that put me in the most danger...

or maybe it was his smile.

The smile that was equally cute and painful,

but I never seemed to mention the painful part.

I was the best at making excuses

for his faults and mine,

but I thought I was right.

People didn't like us together.

And they didn't even see the worst of it.

They didn't know my bruises were from his temper.

He never threw a punch though.

Which is why it took me so long to see it.

Slamming me to the ground or up against a wall to release his

angry energy was his specialty.

I didn't know abuse came in so many shades.

I owe my life to music.

Music is the reason I am still alive today.

Music helped me separate from reality.

Music brought out my true self.

Music helped me forget about all the sadness

back when I didn't know what to live for.

I lived for music.

I'd plan concerts for every month or so.

The goal was to at least make it to that concert,

but by the time that concert would come around

I'd already have tickets to the next one.

So, I'd have to pull through until then.

That is why I am here today.

Music saved my life.

One day I'll find someone who looks at me the way I look at new cities. With passion and wonder, but also a hint of fear.

I want someone to love me the way I love to travel. Always wanting to learn more and experience every little detail.

I want someone to flip through my mind like a thrilling novel yet there is nothing thrilling about me.

Maybe one day I'll be more to someone than I have ever been. Maybe one day I'll be more.

I'm not exactly sad anymore.
At least I don't think so.
I mean I don't necessarily want to die,
but I'm not actively trying to live.
I'm kind of indifferent to living.
That's not suicidal right?
So I'm fine.

Wrong.

When I Started To Have A Clue

People always say:

"To find love, you just need to be yourself."

But I'm not exactly sure how to find her either.

I've never felt lonelier than I did by your side.

During every relationship I've been in, people have always told me:

"You are worth more."

"He shouldn't treat you like that."

"You <u>deserve</u> more."

If so many people see that, why can't the man I love see that?
I'm starting to think I'm not worth more and I deserve to be
treated this way.

Taken for granted. Uncared for. Unloved.

Is that all I'm worth?

It's amazing how much lighter I feel without you.

Anxiety makes me a "psychopath."

Not the type of psychopath who will go kill someone and hide the body as part of their daily routine, but the type who always thinks something is wrong. No matter how "good" things seem.

Sometimes things seem too good to be true. So something must be wrong, right?

If someone doesn't answer for a couple hours or is acting a little less enthusiastic than normal, it is because they lost interest in you or annoyed by you.

In reality, they could be busy or having a rough day, but your brain says, "nope, they hate you." "He's probably cheating or at least thinking about it." "She definitely hates you and is talking behind your back."

Even if someone is fully 100% excited to see you, responding quickly, or just simply enjoys your presence it could be because they want something or are hiding something.

I thought our story was going to be different.

How did the world become so twisted
that a woman demanding respect
is considered "too bold."

Thank you for showing me you are not worth my time.
I don't think I would have seen that on my own.

Thanks to your absence,
I'm more myself than I've ever been.

I can't wait to find the man I thought you were.

Inside an anxious mind

.

.

"I don't fit in with my family."

"I always feel like an outsider."

"She did that on purpose."

"He doesn't like me anymore."

"Sorry."

"Are they trying to break me down?"

"Telling me to 'stop having anxiety' makes me more anxious."

"Nobody gets me."

"Maybe I'm just being a brat."

"Maybe I'm just not meant to be happy."

"I know people have it worse than me."

"I can't just snap out of it."

"What if I looked dumb?"

"They're laughing at me."

"What if he leaves me?"

"What if they find better friends?"

"Nobody should have to deal with me."

"I don't deserve to be happy."

"Nobody likes me here."

"This is it."

"I'm exhausted"

"My whole body hurts."

"I'm going to be sick."

"I can't breathe."

"My vision is fading"

"My body is cold."

"I'm losing my balance."

Blackout.

Anxiety is ordering the easiest thing to say on the menu to lessen your chance of screwing it up, but still practicing how to order it... then not even being able to eat.

I have filled my sinuses just by sniffing up my snot for over an hour because even the thought of having to get up for a tissue or walk in front of the room gave me anxiety.

Anxiety is thinking he doesn't love you and he is losing feelings, even if he just told you he loves you.

Anxiety feels like there is a snake wrapped around your chest and it hurts to breathe.

Anxiety makes me look like I'm never pleased, like I'm a psycho, like I'm needy, like I'm cynical, and like I'm always angry.

Anxiety sounds like those people in the corner are laughing at you. Anxiety sounds like there is always someone in your head reminding you of things to worry about.

Nothing seems to help.

I want to give my body a rest, but I can't sit still. I need to be doing something or I'm wasting time. There's always something I can get a head start on.

I want to be alone, but I want you next to me.

Once a doctor knows you have Generalized Anxiety Disorder, their job is quite simple. Everything else that could ever be wrong with you is "due to the anxiety" and those things won't ever get better until your anxiety gets better. Nothing will even get a second thought.

Anxiety is constant sensory overload even if you're in a quiet, dark room by yourself.

It has been a long time since I've gotten a full breath.

I feel needy a lot of the time. I want you, but I want to be alone. I want to watch a movie, but also read a book, and also take a nap. I want to eat food, and I want to go on a run, and then I want to cry, and then I want to have a party.

It only takes something as simple as a look,

a joke,

or a comment.

One single moment

can keep me up for hours.

...Even if it happened 5 years ago.

I don't want to be the sad quiet one anymore.

Take a second to step back and look at your life.

Are you happy?

Life is not about who you're dating, what job you have, or how much money is in your bank account.

Are YOU Happy?

Do you wake up excited to be living the life you have?

Lately, I find myself not wanting to go to sleep just like we all did as children.

I don't look forward to ending my days anymore.

I don't settle anymore.

I'm no longer focused on how I look or what other people think.

I fill my days with things I love and what makes me happy.

I am happy now.

I feel like by the time I figure out who I really am I won't have any time left to actually be me.

There are still many nights when I want to throw everything away
and pick up a blade for the first time in years.
All because I crave the escape.
I crave the rush.
I crave the release of all the built up frustration.
I crave the first breath of fresh air after the razor leaves its mark.
I crave the feeling of having control.
I'd take physical pain on my skin over the demons that tear
through my head and chest any day.

Instead of cutting I...

Instead of cutting I listen to music. It's not always that easy though. Sometimes my headphones can't overcome the sound of my heartbeat pounding like a steel drum.

Instead of cutting I piece together a puzzle in hopes that my thoughts will follow.

Instead of cutting I sleep, but there is only so much time for sleep. Eventually my body peels my eyelids open just so I can see all of the things around me that cause my anxiety, instead of just having the thoughts infiltrate my every thought.

Instead of cutting myself I cut everyone else off. Part of me hopes it will help keep my thoughts straight and part of me wants some- one to notice I'm gone... And another part of me doesn't.

Instead of cutting I keep both hands occupied because the second one of them is free it will find the nearest, sharpest thing.

Instead of cutting I try to forget the craving. I try to remember how long it has been and why I don't want to ruin that now. It's like being sober. I think about where I could hide the cuts and if anyone would even notice.

I don't like knowing the only reason I'm here is because of a little white pill.

You know, I'm not afraid of darkness; perhaps therein lies the problem.

I no longer fear what would happen if I cross the street without looking.

I'm not a fan of the fact that the only thing that keeps me on the ground as opposed to that magical place in the sky is whether I end up having a good day or a bad one.

That's all changing now, don't you see? The conversation has been started.

I have been finding it harder and harder to pick up a pencil.
I'm not sure if that is a bad thing or a good thing.
I no longer have constant cravings to escape my own body.
I no longer crave the company of absolutely nobody at all times.
Sometimes I even feel like the 300 pound weight on my shoulders
is only 150.
I'm guessing it is a good thing.

I have found it easier to express what I'm feeling,
but maybe that is because what I have been feeling lately is
happiness and relief and all things that make me "easier to be
around" — or so I'm told.

Sometimes I feel like I just don't feel as deeply as I used to
and that just might have to be okay.

Why is it that we always want to be "just like everyone else?"

We fear being different.

Yet, when we describe things that are worth the most, we say they are rare, scarce, or unlike anything you've seen before.

Hell, in that case, I would buy me with every last dollar to my name.

Because the things that identify closest with myself would be the black swan on a beautiful lake surrounded by beautiful, sparkling white ones.

How do I expect someone to be able to handle me if I can't even handle myself?

How do I expect someone to handle me when I don't even know who "me" is?

Today, I listened to some of my old music.

I thought back to the time I had listened to it last.

I started to tear up thinking

I was probably sitting on the bathroom floor

with a blade to my thigh

wishing to end it all.

Then I started to cry harder

thinking about how far I've come since then

and how far I'll go

thanks to God not answering my prayers on those dark days.

Oh boy, have I come a long way.

I'm damn proud of that.

I've learned it is extremely important to let yourself feel
when you need to feel.
When you're happy, feel it.
Let yourself feel happy.
When something hurts you, say it. *Feel it.*
It is okay to feel hurt/sad/mad.
It is *normal* to feel.
That doesn't make you "emotional."
That doesn't make you "hard to handle."
That doesn't make you "weak."
— Because I've heard all of that before

When you don't let yourself feel,
you will go through your days pretending to be bulletproof.
Pretending you are fearless.
Then one day, all of those feelings you never allowed yourself to
feel will come pouring out and you will wonder
how you became so broken.

I am interesting because I am sad and have been broken.
I believe that wholeheartedly.

If I were happy, I wouldn't be able to tell you the intricate
thoughts that run through my head before I go to sleep because I
would just... go to sleep.

I wouldn't be able to tell you how it feels when the first drop of
hot water hits your skin as you enter the shower in the dead of
winter because I would just feel it and move on with my day.

I wouldn't be able to tell you how whole I feel when your hand is
placed in mine because if I weren't sad and broken I would think
that is just how love is supposed to feel and that my love is not
special.

I wouldn't be able to tell you about all forms of joy in exquisite
detail because regular people feel joy almost every day.

Before today, I would have told you to never date a girl with a mental illness. Now I can't think of a reason why not to.

When you pick a flower from the ground to give to her, she will feel like all of her broken pieces have been glued together with gold. A happy girl might only remember that moment for a few moments, giggle, and move on. Because she can.

And one day I'd love to be able to tell you that you can be happy and still feel things the way I do, but you can't.

I don't agree with the things I've done.

Even though the scars are growing thin,

never will I forget that first day I put a razor to my skin.

And if I only knew
all of the struggles were
merely a catalyst for one
        crazy,
              weird,
                    beautiful life.

Now that you can see all of my broken pieces,

do you still love me?

How We
Change The World

One day everything will fall into place. Suddenly you will realize every night you've fallen asleep with tears streaming down your face was part of the journey. You will realize every heartbreak was a step forward on your map. You will smile when the sun comes up. You will smile when the sun goes down. You will smile at fresh flowers and you will smile in the rain. People say you've changed. Truth is, you grew.

You are you
and that is important.

Mental illness is exactly that. It's an illness.

An insidious disease that doesn't leave a mark on your

body—unless you do.

You don't see people telling cancer patients they just need to

toughen up and deal with it. It's all in their head.

You don't see doctors telling amputees their feelings of emptiness

are invalid because they have people surrounding them every day.

But you don't see me crying do you?

I'm not here for pity.

I'm here to start the conversation.

The conversation that has been suppressed for generations.

It has been made clear to me why I'm still able to stand here and

speak to you.

I am in the world to spread awareness.

I am in the world to be a support for those like me who need

somebody.

I am in the world to change the world.

There will be a day when you get home from work,
take a hot shower,
throw your feet up on the coffee table,
and realize you're home.

And you don't need anybody else to make you feel that.

It's unrealistic to think that just you can change the world.

Do it anyway.

Sometimes it feels like you can't face the day on your own.

Do it anyway.

There will be a time you look forward to waking up in the morning. But until then...

Do it anyway.

You'd be out of your damn mind to fall in love with a girl like me.

Do it anyway.

There's nothing I hate more than when people think they would
rather be unhappy with someone than happy on their own.
Happiness is everything.
It's why we wake up every day.
You should wake up to be you.
Not for anything or anyone else.
Wake up to be the best version of yourself you can be.
Wake up to be better than you were yesterday.
Be your own person before being anyone else.

And if you can't say from the deepest part of your being that this
person lights up your entire world, you need a new person.

If there is one thing I've learned in my 22 years,
it is that you can either chase the light
or be the light.

You know, we spend so much time focusing on physical illnesses we forget your brain can be sick too. Countless times I have been told, "oh don't worry it's just a bad week," or " I know, I'm so stressed too."

Anxiety is NOT just stress.

My journey began in 2010. It has been years since I purposely put a mark on my body. The scars have healed and faded, but not a week goes by where I don't struggle to keep it that way. I used to always say, "once you start, you will always have that urge in you," but that stops today. Today I made a promise to myself. From this day forward, I can look here to remind me why I'm fighting.

I spend a lot of my class time writing this book
because I'm one of those students who believes
understanding yourself is more important than what some old guy
thinks about how the world came into existence.
I mean your favorite subject should be yourself, right?
Sometimes I feel like I know more about arrhythmias, spinal cords,
and broken bones than I know about the way my own thoughts
work or who I truly am.
Shouldn't we be taught to become experts on ourselves before we
focus on all the other subjects that are "so important" in life?
If you don't know yourself, how are you supposed to change the
world?

One day I started a list. My list. This list consists of all of the beautiful parts of my world that I would have missed if God had answered my prayers on those dark and lonely nights. Simple things you wouldn't necessarily think about until they were missing. Some of these things are obvious milestones and others are some of the simplest pleasures most people take for granted. On my 21st birthday, I sat in my bed with the only light illumining my damp face being my computer screen. Tears streamed uncontrollably down my cheeks as I opened the document, scrolled to the bottom, and typed, "Turning 21."

Singing in the car with friends

Going to soccer games

Being captain of my soccer team

Getting my black belt

Being in a service club

Prom

Football games

Discovering my dream career

Going to Punta Cana

Attending college

Going to London

Doing service in Honduras

Feeling the warmth of sunlight on your skin when you're cold

Starting nursing clinical

Being an Orientation Assistant

Meeting lifelong friends

Living with new people

Quiet days with a good book

Falling in love with nursing and getting to help people every day

Volunteering at the Montessori Preschool

Helping others with their mental health

Hearing new music by your favorite band

Sunny days on campus

Going on Retreats

Spending time with family

Rudy (my dog)

Leading a service trip to Belize

Lighting a new candle

Studying abroad in Ireland

Feeling proud after getting a good grade

Sitting by a warm fire

Making people's day

Going to concerts

Seeing my friends grow up

Beach days

Turning 21

So here's to us.

Here's to the fighters.

Here's to the silent sufferers.

Here's to the survivors.

Here's to the end of the days you have to pretend like you're asleep so nobody knows you've been crying all day.

Here's to the end of, "oh I'm just tired."

Here's to the end of faking it.

Here's to the supporters.

Here's to the non-judgmental listeners.

Here's to the end of this chapter in life.

Here's to a new beginning.

Here's to happy endings.

40036023R00069

Made in the USA
San Bernardino, CA
23 June 2019